LIES

Other titles in the Hodder African Readers series

Presented to: Laniyan Victoria
By: Stanville School.

A FEW
LITTLE
LIES

By Joanne Bloch

Illustrated by Lois Neethling

HODDER
EDUCATION
PART OF HACHETTE LIVRE UK

© Joanne Bloch 2009
First published in 2009 by
Hodder Education,
Part of Hachette Livre UK,
338 Euston Road
London NW1 3BH

Impression number   5 4 3 2 1
Year   2012 2011 2010 2009 2008

Cover and illustrations by Lois Neethling
Typeset in 13/15 Bembo by RockBottom g&d, KZN, SA
Printed in Great Britain by CPI Cox & Wyman, Reading, RG1 8EX

A catalogue record for this title is available from the British Library

ISBN 978 0340 984154

Chapter One

A strange thing happened to me earlier this year. I forgot how to concentrate. Sometimes it happened at school, and for a while my teachers shouted at me, and tried to make me listen. But soon they gave up – I suppose there were just too many other people to shout at.

At least I managed to concentrate in class sometimes. And occasionally when I wasn't concentrating, it looked as if I was. The real problem came when I needed to study. Every time I sat down with my books, my mind went blank, and I would find myself doodling in the margins, drawing cartoons of hot DJs and celebrities from TV. Or I would start dreaming about my plans to be a big star. Once or twice, I even fell asleep with my head on the table.

Of course, I thought that studying is very boring – so at first I didn't care that I couldn't do it any more. But after a while, I started failing in tests. Mrs Mabena takes my class for quite a few subjects. One day she called me to see her at break.

'Sindiswa, I've noticed that your marks for my subjects are dropping,' she said, peering at me from behind her thick, old-fashioned glasses. There was a pause. I said nothing; I just looked at the floor.

'Is there any reason for this? Has anything happened to upset you?' she asked.

What could I say? My aunt had died, but that was already a few months before, and I tried not to think about her too much any more. Ma didn't speak about her either. So I told Mrs Mabena I was fine. Then I carried on failing . . . and she just seemed to give up on me.

In a way I wished my mom would give up as easily as Mrs Mabena. No chance of that, though! Ma doesn't give up easily. She began asking me when the next test was all the time, and lecturing me about studying. Every time I promised I would study, but then somehow, I didn't. And every time Ma asked me how I had done after a test, and I told her my marks, she looked more and more worried.

Well, I had to do something, didn't I? I remember the first time I cheated in a test. It was a history test − not exactly my favourite subject. But what I remember the best is how surprised I was, because it was so easy. My best friend, Mandisa, sat next to me, and she made sure I could see all her answers. It was as simple as that. Mandisa is a brilliant student, and she knows all her work backwards. She always gets good marks, and she was happy to share some of her brainpower with me. It's obvious Mrs Mabena can't see so well through those thick glasses of hers, so we knew she wouldn't notice – and we were safe from prissy miss Portia because at that time she was sitting right in front.

That was Part One of learning to be dishonest. Part Two was telling my mom how well I'd done in my history test. I thought perhaps she would be surprised, or even suspicious, because I'd been failing for quite a while. But I was wrong. Ma was so happy when I told her I'd got 70 per cent, she nearly burst into tears. She gave me a big hug. 'I knew all along you could do it if you tried,' she said.

When I went to bed that night, I felt like crying myself. What had I done? I'd never told Ma such a big lie before, and I felt terribly guilty. I decided I would never cheat again. I'll study instead, I said to myself. I know I can do well if I try harder. That made me feel better, and I fell asleep.

But only two days later, Mrs Mabena told the class we were going to have a geography test. If there's one subject I hate more than history, it's geography. All those horrible, confusing types of clouds! Who cares about the difference between cirrus and stratus clouds? When I leave school, I'm not planning on being a farmer. I'm going to be an actress on TV – and acting has nothing to do with clouds.

What I'm trying to say is that I hate geography – and somehow, even though I meant to study, the

night before the test I found myself looking at pictures of my favourite actress in a magazine instead.

I felt a little bit nervous at school the next day, but Mandisa came to my rescue again. She didn't even say anything. She just winked at me before the test and, before I knew it, I was copying her. A few days later, I found myself telling Ma all about my good marks for geography.

'This is great news!' said Ma. 'I'm so glad you're finally taking studying more seriously. It's an answer to my prayers.'

I felt guilty again. For the next test, I'll study, I told myself later. Then I'll get good marks because I tried hard, and not because I'm a cheat.

But of course, cheating was so easy now that I did it again. The next time I copied Mandisa for an English vocabulary test, I didn't even feel guilty. Everybody cheats – it's a part of life, I told myself. I can't help it if I have a bad memory.

And by this stage, it was going to be very awkward if I suddenly failed again, just when Ma thought I had turned into a wonderful student. Who wants to upset their mother? Not me – I love my mom. A few little lies won't hurt, I thought, as I copied the word 'definitely' from Mandisa's book. Ma needs me to do well.

In any case, I had other things on my mind. So did Mandisa. Both of us were very excited about the chat room we had discovered that morning.

Chapter Two

'Look at what my dad gave me yesterday, girls,' Mandisa's boyfriend Siya had said early that morning, carefully drawing a brand new, shiny and flat cellphone from the pocket of his blazer. We both gasped in envy.

Before this, we hadn't realised that Siya was rich. He hadn't been at our school for very long, so we didn't know that much about him.

'He talks about church a bit too much,' said Mandisa, pulling a face. 'But don't you think he's good looking?'

I had to agree. Not only was Siya handsome, but he was also tall, and very good at soccer. Mandisa's parents were really strict, so she could only see him at school. They wrote each other little notes every day, and he'd given her a beautiful ring for Valentine's Day. Although the stone wasn't a real gem, it glowed like a ruby, and I was secretly jealous of it.

Before school, Siya showed us all the things his phone could do. First he took a picture of us posing next to the school vegetable garden. Then we made a little video of us doing our special dance. The photo and the video were great – but we were over the moon when he told us how he could use his phone to go into his favourite chat room on the Internet.

Mandisa and I had seen her uncle take photos and make videos on his cellphone. But we didn't know much about chat rooms.

'All I had to do was ask for the address of the chat room from one of the guys in my class, and then type it into my phone,' he explained. 'Now I can log on whenever I want to.'

'But what happens in a chat room?' Mandisa and I asked at the same time, as Siya showed us which buttons to press to log on.

'You chat, of course,' he replied. Then we felt silly and began to giggle.

'How many people have you chatted to so far?' asked Mandisa.

'Not so many – about ten.'

'What were they like?' I asked. 'What did you talk about?'

'Mostly soccer,' replied Siya with a big smile. I could tell he felt quite proud of himself. I understood why – if I had a phone like his, I'd also feel happy. My phone was a big, chunky old brick that my mom bought second hand from her friend at work. Still, it was better than nothing. Mandisa didn't even have a phone. Her parents were very strict and old fashioned, and they didn't really like cellphones.

'At break I'll log on and find someone for you to chat to,' promised Siya, just before school began.

As soon as our test was over and the bell rang, Mandisa and I rushed outside to meet him. He was waiting for us near the gate.

'I'm online already,' he said. 'There are only a few people in the chat room though – let's see, there's Candy, and Doc and Mr T . . . I spoke to Mr T about soccer yesterday. He knows a lot. Let's try him.'

We watched as Siya quickly wrote: *Hey Mr T, what's up?* and pressed send. At that moment, Ridgely and Neo came running up.

'Hurry up, Siya!' shouted Neo. 'We're waiting for you!'

Siya looked blank for a second. Then he remembered.

'Oh, the game!' he said. 'Sorry girls, I have to go – here, keep my phone until after school! Look after it, OK!'

As Siya handed the phone to Mandisa, it tinkled. Mandisa and I grinned at each other. Mr T had replied.

'What does he say?' I asked her.

'I'm cool. How about you?' read out Mandisa. She thought for a second. Then, as I watched, she wrote: *I'm hot enough to warm you up, Baby.*

I gasped. 'Mandisa! You can't send that!'

But Mandisa just laughed.

'Why not?' she asked. 'I'm only having some fun.' And before I could stop her, she added in *By the way, I'm Siya's friend, Mandi*, and pressed the send button.

And just like that, the trouble began.

CHAPTER THREE

I don't know what Mandisa and Mr T talked about that day – but I know it must have been interesting. Mandisa usually can't shut up for a minute. Now suddenly she wouldn't even look at me, never mind talk. Instead, she bent over Siya's phone, sucking in her bottom lip as she punched at its keys. The phone began to tinkle every minute or so, and Mandisa giggled and pulled silly faces and fiddled with her hair as she read Mr T's replies. After a while, I felt bored with just sitting and looking at her as if she were some new kind of reality TV show, and went over to talk to Pinky and Natasha, who were having their lunch nearby.

It took only half an hour for Mandisa to fall for Mr T. That's one thing you have to say about the guy – he's very good at charming people! By the end of that break, Mandisa was crazy about him – and she'd never even seen him. Poor Siya had suddenly gone right out of fashion.

'Siya's nice,' Mandisa said, as we walked into class after break, 'but he's too childish. Mr T is a real man! He makes me feel special!'

When we met Siya after school, Mandisa hardly looked at him. 'Bye,' she said, in an offhand way, as she handed him his phone. 'See you tomorrow.'

'So —' said Siya, but Mandisa was already walking out of the school gates, flicking her braids as she went. As I followed her, I looked back for a moment, and saw Siya standing there, looking slightly confused.

Poor Siya! I wanted to slap Mandisa. I wanted to tell her that a great guy like Siya deserved a chance; for one thing, he was a real live person, not just some words on a screen.

'What about the ring he gave you?' I wanted to ask. 'You're still wearing it on a chain around your neck, remember? What about the way you said you'd never, ever take it off?'

But before I could say any of this, Mandisa had me thinking about something else altogether.

'Sindi, you know how I've been helping you with your tests?' she began.

I nodded. Of course I knew.

'Well,' she went on, 'I think it's time you paid me back.' I stared at her with a funny feeling in my stomach.

'But Mandisa . . .' I started saying, but she carried on talking as if I hadn't said a word.

'You know how happy it's made your mom,' she said.

'You wouldn't want to disappoint her again, would you?'

12

She had me there, and we both knew it.

'OK,' I said with a sigh. 'How do you want me to pay you back?'

'Just lend me your phone for a while,' said Mandisa. 'I'll buy the airtime, don't worry. I need to stay in touch with Mr T.'

I stared at her in disbelief. She knew how much I loved my phone. How could she expect me to hand it over, just because it suited her?

'That's not fair!' I said, but she ignored this, and held out her hand.

'But ... but ... what if my mom finds out!' I said in a whiny, pathetic voice. I knew it was no good though. Mandisa always gets what she wants.

'Sindi, she won't. And you know I need it more than you do!'

What could I say? Sadly, I handed Mandisa my phone.

'I just hope Ma won't notice,' I said in a sulky voice, but Mandisa didn't even hear me. She was staring at the sky with a faraway look in her eyes and a small smile on her lips. There was no doubt about it – Mandisa was hooked.

Chapter Four

Mandisa probably had a great time writing messages to her new love interest for hours and hours that evening. It was a bit different for me. Somehow, not having my phone around made me feel lonely. This was silly, I suppose, because I hardly ever had airtime anyway, and when I did, I only sent one or two messages to my cousin in Jo'burg every few days. Still, I missed my phone.

Ma was on a late shift that week, so she was only due home at nine o'clock.

At about six o'clock, my little sister Dudu came to find me. 'I'm hungry,' she said. 'Come and help me cook,' But I just glared at her.

'Go away!' I said. 'It's still too early to make supper, and you know it's your turn, anyway.'

'Well, I helped *you* last week when it was your turn,' she whined, but I didn't want to listen.

'Just shut up, Dudu!' I said in a loud voice. 'Didn't you hear me telling you to GO AWAY?'

'I'll tell Ma you're being rude to me!' I could hear her bleating as she walked away, but I took no notice.

For a while I sat in the bedroom, half-heartedly doing my homework, but stopping to stare out the window every now and then. Not that I could see much – only a stunted old guava tree, and behind it a fence that had always looked as if it were about to fall over. When the last light left the sky, I couldn't even see that any more. Somehow the darkness made me feel even worse. I closed the curtains, but being alone was so bad that I went to hang out with Dudu in the kitchen after all. I helped her cook a little bit. Well, I washed the potatoes.

Dudu was only eleven, and I thought she was really boring. For quite a while I had tried very hard just to ignore her – she always seemed to talk about such stupid, childish stuff. But that night, something about the sad look in her big round eyes made me listen when she suddenly said, 'It's Ma's birthday this month. Do you remember her birthday last year?'

I thought for a second. Then I said, 'Yes, what about it?'

'Nothing,' she replied. 'It was just nice.'

After that, I turned on the radio and sang along to all the songs. I tried to think of nothing much while I sang. Not my cellphone that was gone and how frustrated I was with Mandisa and how trapped I was. And I tried not to think of Auntie Patience either. But I couldn't help it – sometimes it's hard not to remember.

I knew exactly what Dudu was talking about, and although I didn't want to, I started remembering Ma's birthday the year before. I thought of how Auntie Patience helped us cook a big meal as a surprise for Ma. It was all ready by the time she came home – chicken, rice, butternut and beans. We had tinned peaches and cream, because Ma loves them, and Auntie Patience had made a chocolate birthday cake, with candles on it. I remembered how we sang happy birthday, and how Auntie Patience laughed when Ma blew out the candles . . . but then I just couldn't bear to remember any more, so I sang louder, and started dancing too. I was still dancing when our tired-looking mother finally walked in.

Chapter Five

'Guess what he told me last night?'

These were Mandisa's first words every time she saw me for the next few days. Then she would whip out my phone, and read me the messages.

I had mixed feelings about this. I still felt angry that she'd taken my phone, and I was sorry for Siya too. I also felt a tiny bit jealous – nobody had ever sent me messages like that, and it felt as if nobody ever would.

But it was also fun hearing the latest messages. Mr T definitely had a way with words, and his messages were very flattering. *Baby, u make me swoon!!! u r so fresh and sexy!!* began one message.

I interrupted her there. 'How does he know? He hasn't even met you!'

But Mandisa just shrugged her shoulders, and carried on reading. *u r my sun, my moon and all the stars in the sky*, she read in a smirky voice. *I think of u as a red rosebud*, he told her the next day, but only a day later she had become *my tiger lily, more gorgeous than any beauty queen.*

Then he started on the gifts he was going to buy her. A diamond necklace to wear on her swan-like neck, with matching earrings for her seashell ears. A bag from Paris, because she deserved the best. Shoes from New York that would show off her gorgeous feet. (We both laughed about that one – the soles of Mandisa's feet were like a riverbed in the middle of a long drought.)

Mandisa, as usual, was very generous. 'You know, Sindi,' she said, 'he's going to give me so much stuff that I'll be able to share some of it with you.'

Then there were the gadgets, the things Mr T was going to buy Mandisa to keep her happy. He was big on music, especially R&B and hip-hop, so the first thing on his list was a CD player, and a few hundred CDs. A top of the range iPod would follow.

Baby, would u like a nice big flat-screen TV with surround sound speakers 2 watch in bed? he asked one day. The thought of Mandisa's father allowing her even the tiniest TV in her bedroom made me laugh.

'He doesn't mean now, though,' explained Mandisa patiently. 'He means later on, you know, when we're together.'

Somehow the messages never said much about Mr T himself. He only told her that his name was Trevor, and that he was a few years older than she was.

'Where does he live?' I asked her once.

'Oh ... I don't think he lives very far away,' she replied, vaguely.

'What school does he go to?'

'Don't be silly, Sindi!' she snapped. 'That's not important! The thing is, we're in love – the details just don't matter.'

It was fun to hear Mandisa read out Mr T's messages, but I really missed my phone. It seemed so unfair – why should I have to lose my precious phone, just so she could communicate with her stupid boyfriend? But I knew there was nothing I could say, so I just stared at my phone sadly, and prayed every night that it would stay safe. Actually, there was nothing to worry about – Mandisa was looking after that old brick as if it were made of 24-carat gold. She knew she had to be very careful about hiding it away; if her parents saw her using it, there would be big trouble.

'I always keep it on silent,' she told me, 'and we only send messages when my parents are fast asleep.'

As for Siya, Mandisa paid him just enough attention to keep him hanging on – but not enough for him to relax.

'Hi Baby,' she would say, when she saw him, but somehow it sounded cold, as if she wasn't really pleased to see him. She stopped taking his hand all the time, and going to watch him play soccer after school. We also stopped sitting at our usual place on the edge of the vegetable garden at break, and moved to different corners of the school grounds every day, so it was hard for him to find us.

Poor guy – he was very brave. He never complained about having to search for us all over the place, and when he did manage to find us, he would look pleased and greet us with a happy smile. Of course, this just irritated Mandisa.

'He's like a big puppy!' she would say as soon as he was far enough away from us not to hear. 'He's just too friendly all the time! He's too sweet!'

I felt really sorry for him. Although he didn't say anything about the way she was treating him, I could sometimes see in his eyes that he felt hurt and confused. Once or twice I imagined telling him about Mr T, but how could I? Mandisa was my best friend. We'd known each other since the first day of Grade 1, so we'd had a long time to work out what we expected from each other. Once, in Grade 5, Mandisa told this other girl, Tiny, that I secretly called her Fishface. Tiny punished me for that by bashing me on the head with her school bag and stamping hard on both my feet. After that, I wouldn't speak to Mandisa for at least two weeks, and when I finally did, we agreed that we would never, ever tell anyone each other's secrets again.

And anyway, telling Siya that Mandisa was interested in somebody else would hurt his feelings. I couldn't bear to do that!

CHAPTER SIX

'Yaaah! Hey! Over here, Sifiso! Waah! WATCH OUT!'

It was Friday, everybody's favourite day, and I could already hear a big group of boys bellowing and laughing raucously from far away as I neared our school. There was no mistaking the Friday feeling in the air – as if all the animals in the zoo were waiting to be let out of their cages for a special treat.

As I entered the school gates, there was a loud whooshing noise, and I had to duck to avoid a tennis ball whizzing past my ear. 'Hello Sindi!' shouted Crazy Charles, as he leapt to catch it. He was gone long before I could reply.

I pushed patiently through crowds of shrieking, laughing girls and guys as I made my way down to the mulberry tree, where Mandisa was waiting for me.

As soon as she saw me, she started talking very fast. 'Guess what! Guess what! He called last night!'

The early mornings are a funny time for me. It's not that I feel grumpy like some people. My mom, for example – every morning it's the same: 'Wake up!

Get up! Get dressed! Hurry up! Brush your teeth!'
until we finally rush out of the front door, just so
we can escape. And my aunt was always tired in the
morning, yawning while she boiled the kettle for
her coffee. But I don't feel tired – I'm usually wide-
awake as soon as I open my eyes. I definitely feel
quiet, though, and I like to walk to school alone, so
that I don't have to talk.

So that morning, even though I was surrounded
by hundreds of cackling, jostling, shouting lunatics,
my mind was still far away. It took me a moment to
understand what Mandisa was talking about.

'Who called?' I asked stupidly.

'What do you mean, "Who called"? Who do you
think called?' said Mandisa impatiently, but she was
too happy to be irritated. In fact, she was grinning
like a big, silly idiot.

'His voice is *so* sexy – kind of deep and growly
– I nearly fainted! We spoke for almost an hour! And
guess what again! I'm going to meet him tomorrow
afternoon in town!'

'But how?' I asked. 'I mean, your parents —'

Mandisa smiled at me sweetly. 'You're going to
help me of course! Remember we have a biology
test today?'

I nodded, dumbly.

'You want to do well in it, don't you?' she went
on.

I nodded again.

'So I guess you'll give me a little help in return, won't you?'

I stared at her. I wanted to talk, but no words came out of my mouth. Inside my head, though, just for a second or two, I was saying no. No, this has to stop. No, cheating is wrong, and I don't want to do it any more. No, I won't help you lie to your parents. That's a bad thing to do...

But Mandisa was right. There was another test that day; in fact, the bell was ringing and it was about to begin. Although I quite like biology and I'd tried to study for about seven pathetic minutes the night before, I knew I hadn't taken much in. It was my turn to cook, anyway, so I was too busy to learn. And I didn't want my mom to feel worried about me. And really, it was very kind of Mandisa to help me with my tests, so perhaps I should help her, just this one, last time.

'OK,' I said finally. 'What do you want me to do?'

CHAPTER SEVEN

It turned out I didn't have to do much, only tell Ma that Mandisa and I needed to work on our history project together, and ask if she could sleep over on Saturday night. Ma said yes quite happily – she loved hearing the words 'work' and 'history' in the same sentence. I was happy too, because I wasn't really lying – only not telling Ma that Mandisa's mom thought she was at our house all afternoon.

Mandisa, of course, was the happiest of all of us. 'I just wish our date could be a bit longer,' she said, 'but T doesn't want me travelling about all alone when it's dark. He wants me to be safe – he's very protective, you know.'

Saturday arrived. The morning passed by quite quickly, but the afternoon felt endless. It was a hot, still day. Ma was sleeping – it was all she ever seemed to do when she wasn't at work, which was most of the time. Dudu was playing quietly with her dolls in the shade in the back yard. Every now and then I would hear her murmuring as she changed their outfits, and made them act out the silly stories she was always dreaming up.

A few weeks earlier I'd tried to tell her that it

was time for her to grow up a little and throw those stupid old dollies away, but she didn't want to listen. She just looked at me in an infuriating way. She seemed to be thinking about it. 'No, I like my dolls,' she said in the end. What can you do with a child like her? She'll probably still be sitting on my mom's lap when she's 22.

So there I was, all alone, trying not to think about Mandisa's adventure, and checking the hands of the kitchen clock, which suddenly seemed to be on strike. I was actually trying to do a pile of ironing, but now it seemed I couldn't even concentrate on household tasks any more. Anyway, it was just too hot to iron. After about 15 slow, sweaty minutes, in which I managed to iron two school shirts very badly, I decided to give up for a while and go and lie on my bed.

It was hot in the bedroom too. A fat fly buzzed annoyingly against the windowpane. Why can flies never get out of windows? I asked myself. For a moment I stared at the harsh blue sky above the roof of the neighbours' house, but it was just too bright. I closed my eyes. It was about three o'clock by now, so Mandisa and Mr T would be sitting in McDonald's. I wondered what Mr T looked like. I imagined a boy version of some glamorous, well-built singer-type guy with a perfect six-pack, like you see on TV. Were they staring into each other's eyes, and holding hands? I imagined Mandisa sauntering towards him like a model, flicking her hair and smiling her confident, flirtatious smile. It wasn't fair! Mandisa was so popular with boys! Compared to her, I was a nobody. Here I was, ready and waiting – but recently it was as if my life had gone into a love drought, and there was just no love around.

It's not as if I'm ugly, or anything, I said to myself. OK, I had a few pimples every now and then, but nothing compared to Tulasizwe or Natasha. No! Compared to poor Natasha, my skin was good enough for a huge billboard advertising skin cream. And my features were quite nice too. I knew I had a good figure – so what was it that was wrong about me? Did I smell horrible? I didn't think so – I spent ages every day washing and keeping myself clean and fresh.

Perhaps my hair is ugly, I said to myself. I frowned, and sat up briefly to stare at my hair in the mirror next to my bed. The strange thing was, though, that my hair looked pretty good . . . I sighed and lay down again. It must be my personality, then. Did nobody notice me these days because I was just too quiet at school?

This year, Valentine's Day had been a disaster for me. Almost everybody in my grade seemed to receive a card – except for Stanley the loser and me. (You'd have to be pretty desperate to want Stanley for your valentine. Not that he would notice, one way or another – he was in love with his maths books, the poor boy.) An incredibly handsome Grade 12 guy had given Lethabo a red rose, and even pimply Natasha was given a cute little teddy bear with a red ribbon round its neck by someone or other. But me? I got a big, round zero. And having to listen to Mandisa gush about the ring that Siya had given her didn't exactly help me to feel better either.

To add the final touch to the awful, shameful day, when I arrived home, even Dudu was clutching a card! 'Who gave it to you?' I asked her, trying to sound bored. But if Dudu knew, she wasn't going to tell. She just smirked at me, and turned around to leave the room. 'I got tons of them when I was your age,' I told her as she pranced off. 'I didn't know what to do with them all.'

Actually that was true – I definitely received two or three valentine cards the year I was 11, even if they were just from silly little kids in my class. So what was wrong with me now that I was nearly 15?

By this stage, I was feeling really sorry for myself. The fly was still battling away at the window, and the room was so hot and stuffy that I could hardly breathe. I knew I should get up and do something else, perhaps go outside or even start the horrible history project. At the very least, I should open the window. But it was all too much trouble. So I rolled over to face the wall, and started thinking about my private soapie instead.

Chapter Eight

'And how are you doing today, Miss Njinge?' asked handsome Doctor Dube, taking my poor bandaged hands tenderly into his own warm, strong hands, and gently beginning to unwrap them.

'Oh, healing well,' I said with a brave and dignified smile.

'Yes, they are! What wonderful news!' said Dr Dube in his rich, deep voice. 'Perhaps we should go out to celebrate tonight?'

I kept my private soapie for times when I was very bored, like when Mrs Mabena was explaining about the Industrial Revolution. It also cheered me up when I was feeling sad or gloomy. There was a huge cast, but I was the star of the show, always at the centre of whatever drama was going on.

I was more grown up in the soapie, of course, and stunning to look at. I was a famous actress, with thousands of adoring fans who lived only for my appearances. Wherever I went, they asked for my autograph. It became quite tiring sometimes. Then my bodyguards would have to tell them firmly:

'Give Miss Njinge a bit of space, please. The star needs some room to breathe!'

Now I was in my mansion, waiting for my date to arrive. Dr Dube was a famous surgeon, who saved lives with his daring operations. He had just made the headlines again for performing heart transplants on a pair of twin babies I bravely rescued from a fire I had spotted as my limo passed by. That's when I had burnt my hands a little.

I was just putting the final touches to my make-up when the front doorbell rang. I rose gracefully from my dressing table, and swayed to the entrance hall on my glittering silver high heels. I opened the door. 'Good evening,' I said in a low, sexy voice. There he stood, wearing a fine, soft, beautifully cut cream suit, and carrying a bunch of deep red roses . . . I looked searchingly into his melting brown eyes – but wait a minute! It was Siya!

I blinked. How did that happen? Somehow I'd managed to imagine Siya as the glamorous Dr Dube! I'd never allowed real people into my private soapie before, only me as I was going to be in a few years' time. Siya had to go. I closed my eyes, and tried again – but he wouldn't go away. Every time I thought about Dr Dube, Siya's face would pop up. After a while, I stopped trying to fight it. Actually, Siya's face was beautiful, especially his eyes. Why had I never noticed that before?

Perhaps because he was Mandisa's boyfriend, not yours, you idiot! I said to myself. He still is, actually . . . Or maybe he isn't any more, because of Mr T . . . Who knows what's really going on?

Anyway, Siya's eyes *were* lovely, and perhaps if I could ever find a reason to talk to him, I would be able to look at them again; the thought made me feel happy. The fly at the window buzzed and buzzed, and I fell into a deep sleep.

CHAPTER NINE

I didn't hear much about the date that day. When Mandisa finally arrived, either Ma or Miss Big Ears was always nearby. And actually we really did have a project to do – not that I did much. As usual, Mandisa had done most of it already. I just passed her the glue and the ruler, and coloured in the map.

I was sure the date had gone well, though, because Mandisa was very cheerful; she made silly jokes and giggled a lot. Once when we were alone for a minute, she whispered something in my ear, but the only word I caught was 'hot' before Dudu came to tell us it was dinner time. I thought Mandisa might talk to me when we went to bed, once we could hear that Dudu was sleeping, but she was fast asleep about a minute after I put the light out.

'Can I miss church today, so we can finish our project?' I asked my mother the next morning. (This was another lie – it was already completely finished.)

'Of course you can,' said Ma, looking relieved to have such a studious daughter.

After the usual ironing marathon and fussing about with Dudu's crazy, disobedient hair, I finally heard the front door closing.

'OK! Tell me everything!' I said.

Actually, although Mandisa babbled on and on about Trevor, I really didn't hear anything very new or interesting. It was just the typical stuff, the kind of things you hear girls saying at school every day of the week. Trevor was gorgeous; he was incredibly sexy; he had a dazzling smile; his voice was like a rap star's; his clothes were the coolest... and he treated her like a queen. He'd bought her a great meal, and he'd given her a tiny bottle of the most expensive perfume. Best of all, he'd given her a ring.

'It's not some cheap trashy rubbish out of a lucky packet, like Siya's ring, either!' she said proudly, as she fished about in her bag, and pulled out a little box. She opened it, and I gasped. I could hardly believe Mandisa's luck. The ring sat snugly in its red velvet case. It was gold, with three sparkling little stones embedded in it. It wasn't huge, but somehow its modest size made it seem even more impressive, more tasteful and adult.

'It's perfect!' I said softly.

'Diamonds!' said Mandisa, with a huge, proud grin.

'Real diamonds?'

'Of course! Do you think Trevor is cheap or something?'

I thought for a minute. 'But how could he afford it?' I asked. 'I mean, he's only a school boy, isn't he?'

Mandisa giggled. 'Actually, it turns out he's a bit older than we are – that's probably why he always seemed so mature!'

I'd thought that Mr T was maybe 18 or 19 at the most. Even that seemed old to me, definitely too old for us. Mandisa was actually younger than me by a few months.

There was a small pause. I didn't really want to find out how old Trevor was; the whole subject made me feel nervous. But I knew I had to.

'How old is he?' I asked.

'Oh, he's 27,' she said casually.

I gasped. 'Mandisa! That's old! He's a grown up man!'

But Mandisa just smiled in a superior way. 'I know he's a man, Sindi,' she said. 'That's why I like him.' She took one last look at the ring, and then snapped the case shut and popped it back inside her bag.

'But —' I said and then stopped. It was no use. Mandisa can be very stubborn, and her face had the haughty, closed-off look that I knew so well. It was clear that she had nothing more to say, except that she was going to meet Trevor again the next Saturday morning between nine and twelve.

'It's a pity it has to be so short, but Trevor's got *so* much work to do. His job is very demanding,' she told me. 'Anyway, my cousins are coming to visit in the afternoon, and I have to be at home . . . I'll tell my parents that I'm meeting you in town because we need to buy that new biology book.' She looked at me in a meaningful kind of way. 'That seems like a good plan, don't you think?'

I nodded slowly. There was a sick feeling in my stomach. 'Very good,' I said.

Chapter Ten

'Here in Africa, global warming will affect us very badly,' said Mrs Mabena. 'Can anybody explain why?'

'We'll all get too sweaty,' said Charles.

'Yes, and then the whole of Africa will get very stinky!' shouted Neo.

It was geography, the first lesson on a Monday morning. My concentration was even worse than usual. While Mrs Mabena droned on, and Neo and Charles behaved stupidly as they always did, my mind went round and round until I felt exhausted and confused.

I didn't like the sound of this Trevor guy, not at all. I didn't trust him. How could Mandisa be so stupid? He was too old for her, too old by at least ten years. Perhaps I wasn't the greatest student this world has ever seen, but even an idiot can see that there's something seriously wrong with a 27-year-old man wanting to date a 14-year-old girl. There were explanations of course, and they weren't pretty. Mandisa might be more popular and more experienced than I am, but she wasn't as experienced as she made out, and I knew she wasn't ready for what was bound to happen with this guy. I just couldn't let this romance carry on – but how could I stop it?

The pressure was on. There were only a few days to sort out the problem, because the more Mandisa saw of Mr T, the more she would love him, and the easier it would be for him to persuade her to do anything at all. So what was I going to do? Trying to persuade her that he was too old for her was useless. Mandisa loved this creep way too much to listen to me . . . unless I could somehow prove that he wasn't such a good person after all. But how? Surely there must be a way!

Maybe I could ask somebody to help me. But who? The idea of speaking to Mandisa's mom was almost too horrible to think about. She was a woman who should be living in another century, or perhaps even on another planet. If she found out that her daughter was secretly dating some man off the Internet she might faint, or something. Maybe her hair would turn white overnight. Also, if Mandisa's parents found out about Trevor, she would get into the most terrible trouble. She'd probably be grounded forever, and have to wash dishes until she was at least twenty-one. However she was punished, she was bound to get me back by telling about my cheating; then I'd be in terrible trouble too.

Maybe I should tell Ma – but it was so hard to talk to her. She got worried so quickly and that irritated and upset me. And when she was worried, she shouted, and then I wanted to shout back. If only Auntie Patience were still alive! She was such a good listener, and she always knew what to do. I felt a dull pain in my throat, but I swallowed hard and shook my head slightly. Stop it, Sindiswa, I said sternly to myself inside my head. Now is not a good time to feel sad! You have important work to do.

I looked up. Mrs Mabena was just turning around to write another sentence about climate change on the board. At that moment, Mandisa's hand shot out from the next desk, and a tiny folded up note appeared on my lap. I opened it, and read: *Dumped Siya. Sent him an sms last night. Just can't bear having him hanging around any more.*

Siya! Of course! He was the perfect person to talk to! Why hadn't I thought of him before? He was a bit older than me, but not too much older, and he knew Mandisa. I was sure he would know what to do. The timing isn't exactly great, I thought. Mandisa has just broken up with him, less than 24 hours ago. He may be feeling angry, or upset, and now I'm going to make it all worse by telling him about Mr T.

But he seemed like such a kind, good person. Surely he would see how important it was to help me stop Mandisa from doing this dangerous thing? There was only one way to find out, and I decided it was definitely worth a try.

I turned, and smiled at Mandisa. 'Good, I'm glad,' I whispered.

CHAPTER ELEVEN

It was a good thing I had become such a wonderful liar, because I had to use a bit of cunning to escape from Mandisa at the end of school that day. 'I've decided to join the choir, so I'm staying at school late this afternoon for a practice,' I told Mandisa at break that day.

'The choir?' She stared at me in disgust and disbelief.

'How much singing can one girl do?' She knew I was in the choir at church already, you see.

'My mom wants me to join because I can sing so well,' I mumbled, acting embarrassed. That shut Mandisa up, because she knew singing was one of the few things I could do better than she could. She shrugged her shoulders, and started rambling on about Trevor again.

Endless dreary lessons followed, and I can't say I took much notice of what was going on in any of them. I do remember that Mrs November shouted at me in maths though, because, big surprise, I wasn't listening to her description of the difference between volume and area. (Can anyone in their right mind really blame me?) School seemed to take even longer than usual, but finally we heard the very best sound in the whole world – the last bell of the day.

I packed my books away slowly, trying to think what I was going to say to Siya. I felt a churning, queasy feeling in my stomach. What if he was horrible to me? What if he made fun of me in front of his friends, so that they laughed at me? What if he wouldn't even speak to me, because I was Mandisa's friend, and she had just broken up with him?

I knew exactly where to find Siya. I walked slowly down towards the dusty strip of ground that was our soccer field, where a group of boys had gathered. They hadn't begun playing yet. Instead, they were standing around chatting with a few of their friends. I didn't know any of them, except for the awful Neo, and I felt shy to go any closer. I began to walk even slower, but as soon as Siya saw me, he came over.

'Hi Sindi, What's up?' he said. He didn't look very friendly. 'Has Mandisa sent you to explain why she dumped me?'

'No,' I said, avoiding his eyes, 'not exactly . . . but I do want to talk to you about Mandisa. Do you have any time before your game?'

'That depends . . . Why should I talk about her? She doesn't want anything to do with me any more.'

'I'm worried about her. I think she's in trouble,' I said. 'I need your help – please Siya!'

Siya thought about this. Then he nodded. 'OK,' he said, 'but we can't be long.' Then he shouted over his shoulder, 'Start without me, guys,' and we walked off together, back towards the school building.

That's how I came to be walking around the school grounds with the fabulous Dr Dube, the most famous heart surgeon in Africa, also known as Siya, the boy I had a giant, overwhelming crush on all of a sudden. If I'd stared into his beautiful eyes, I might have become all shy and tongue-tied, but I was too busy telling him how the evil Mr T was trying to seduce our friend to think about my feelings for a while.

Chapter Twelve

At first, when I told Siya that Mandisa was in love with someone else, he just looked hurt and angry; but when I told him it was Mr T, Trevor, the guy from the chat room, and how old he was, Siya was shocked. In fact, he went a bit crazy. I won't write down what he called Trevor, or what he threatened to do to him. Even the perfect gentleman Dr Dube loses it sometimes! But eventually he calmed down enough for us to talk some more.

'What do you think we should do?' he asked, once I had finished telling him all the details I knew.

'Well,' I replied. 'I know they're going to meet in town on Saturday morning. Perhaps we can work out a way of stopping them, or something?'

Siya frowned and rubbed at his forehead. 'I wonder . . . ' he said, scratching his neck and pulling a funny face. 'Let's think now . . . this all started with the chat room.'

At that moment, I had the most brilliant idea. 'Let's log on,' I said, 'and pretend to be Mandisa! We could say that she thinks it's getting too serious too fast – maybe we could even say she's decided he's too old for her!'

'Great idea!' said Siya. 'But I have an even better one – why don't we just cancel the date? She won't know, of course, and when Saturday comes round, and she goes to meet him, he won't appear. Then she'll be angry with him, and that will be the end of the whole thing!'

Siya and I were thrilled with our plan. He pulled his phone out of his pocket, and logged on right that minute. 'I just hope that pervert's online,' he said. He peered into the glow of the screen. 'Yes, he's there,' he said, excitedly. 'Look!' and he pointed at Mr T's name. 'Now what shall we say?'

That was easy enough – I knew exactly how they talked to each other.

'Hi Angel', I said, and Siya typed it in. 'I'm so disappointed Baby . . . I can't make it on Saturday. Will you forgive me?' But Siya was only beginning to write 'disappointed' when I realised that our plan was fatally flawed, and was sure to fail. 'Oh no,' I groaned miserably. 'Siya, you may as well stop. It's not going to work!'

He looked up, surprised. 'But why not? It seems so perfect.'

'It would be perfect, except that Mandisa has my phone, and he calls her every night now.'

'Oh.' Looking disappointed, Siya deleted what he had written and logged off. He put his phone back in his pocket, and we stood quietly for a moment. Then he said, 'OK, well we'll just have to try something else. We still have a few days. I'll think about it later, and you think about it too. Can you meet me at the same time tomorrow?'

I looked up into his perfect eyes. Suddenly I felt kind of shy. 'OK,' I said softly. 'I'll try.'

I have to admit that although we hadn't worked out how to get rid of Trevor, as I walked home, I felt happier and happier. Slowly, deliciously, I let my mind play back what had happened between Siya and me . . . and now we had a reason to meet again the next day! Of course, a more sensible part of me knew that I was being silly – Siya probably still loved Mandisa, and hoped to get her back. But I couldn't help it. I preferred not to be sensible. It was far more fun to let my imagination go wild; so I did just that, all the way home. In fact, I even sang a few of my favourite R&B songs while I was about it, and as I sang, I imagined Siya listening and staring at me with a look of wonder and appreciation on his face.

'Oh Sindi,' I imagined him saying, 'The way you can sing!' I smiled modestly, and held his gaze for a few seconds, and then I sang a little more.

Chapter Thirteen

My mom was on the early shift that week, which put her in a better mood. Or perhaps my own happiness made me see everything differently. Dudu picked up the mood, and was very talkative.

'Mrs Xaba caught two boys cheating today,' she said, while we were washing up after supper that night. 'Cheating is such an ugly thing, isn't it?'

I knew immediately that this wasn't a topic I wanted to discuss very much; it would definitely spoil the atmosphere. Unfortunately, Ma seemed interested. 'What happened to them?' she asked.

'They're in big, big trouble!' said Dudu with relish, but before she could say anything else, I decided it was time to change the subject.

'Ma,' I said, 'can you remember the first time you were in love?'

To my relief, Ma smiled, and seemed to forget all about the cheaters and their horrible punishment. Her busy hands stopped drying for a minute and she said, 'Of course! That's not something anyone would ever forget. Your father had such style! I thought he was the most handsome man I'd ever seen!'

I knew exactly how she must have felt.

'How did you meet?' I asked.

'Through your Aunt Patience,' she said. Her face went sad and serious for a moment. 'It's hard to believe she's gone too now,' she said quietly. 'It was bad enough losing him so suddenly when he was still so young.'

Then she started remembering again. 'Your dad loved to dance,' she told us, smiling again. 'I was always sneaking off to nightclubs with him – my parents were so strict!'

'Nightclubs?' I asked in amazement. 'You went to *nightclubs*?'

She looked at me with raised eyebrows and allowed herself to smile again. 'Yes, my girl, nightclubs. I wasn't your age, though. I was a working woman in my twenties already, after all!'

'OK, I understand,' I nodded, 'but will you let me go to nightclubs one of these days too?'

'Oh yes,' said Ma, 'when you're in your twenties, I will!'

'Ma!' I said crossly, 'That's not fair! Things are different these days!' But then I looked at her, and saw that she was teasing me. 'All in good time, Sindi,' she said.

'I want to go to nightclubs too,' said Dudu suddenly, and all three of us began to laugh. Then Dudu grabbed me and pretended we were a soppy couple dancing. We started laughing and couldn't stop then, and in the end Ma had to send us to bed to have some peace and quiet.

★ ★ ★

Disco lights flashed red and green and loud, crazy music thumped and pounded. All around me, glistening bodies dressed in skimpy glittering clothes swirled and throbbed.

'Baby I love you,' whispered Siya hoarsely into my ear.

'Oh Siya . . . ' I murmured, staring adoringly at his dreamy face, but before I could say anything more, there was a sudden shrill ringing noise.

'No more time!' shouted Siya, looking frantic. 'There's no more time! We must save Mandisa! Come on, Sindi, run! *Run!*' I tried to push my way through the crowd of dancers. It wasn't easy, though – none of them took any notice of me, and when I tried to ask them to let me pass, it felt as if I'd forgotten how to speak. I began to lose sight of Siya.

'Siya,' I croaked desperately, 'please wait for me.'

'Who's Siya?' asked Dudu in a confused sleepy voice. I opened my eyes, and leaned over to turn off the alarm.

'Nobody,' I replied. 'Just a boy in my dreams.' I rolled over, and for the last few minutes before I got up, I thought about the dream. I decided it was telling me something important – that even though I was falling in love with Siya, I had some urgent business to take care of before I could allow myself to think about it. I realised that I'd been so busy thinking about Siya that I had completely forgotten to work on a plan of action for the Mandisa problem.

Then another worrying thought came to me. How on earth was I going to shake Mandisa off so I could meet Siya that afternoon? I was actually feeling almost tired of telling lies all the time – but it looked as if I was going to have to come up with another one.

'Girls!' came a loud, harsh voice from outside the room. 'Time to get up!' The door flew open then, and 'Get up!' said Ma again grimly before she stomped off to the kitchen as she did every morning. I rolled my eyes and sighed loudly. 'OK, get up Dudu, or she'll drive us mad.'

'Ungh,' grunted Dudu regretfully, getting out of bed slowly as she always does, as though she's at least a hundred years old.

Chapter Fourteen

'Give it here! Give it HERE!' screamed Neo, but Charles just brayed like a donkey and galloped off. Class hadn't even begun yet, but the two pests were at it already, trying to wrestle a picture of some woman in a tiny bikini from each other.

'Stop it!' squealed prissy Portia, as Charles leapt past her desk, sending her precious dictionary flying into the air. It hit Dineo hard on her knee.

'Ouch!' she screamed, swatting at Charles, but he took no notice. Instead he waved the picture about, snatching it away just in time as the furious Neo grabbed for it over Stanley's desk, while the maths genius cowered anxiously in the corner.

It wasn't even a Friday, just an ordinary, boring old Tuesday; but somehow, my class was wild that day. Neo and Charles shut up for a while when Mrs Mabena came in, but while she was trying to hand out some history worksheets, they began careering around the classroom again. Mrs Mabena is quite patient, actually, but finally, when Neo snatched at the picture and tore it in half, and then swore loudly and smacked Charles in the chops, she lost her temper. 'Get out!' she said furiously, and off they went to the principal's office. The rest of that lesson was peaceful enough for me to drift off and stare out of the window, while in the background I could dimly hear Mrs Mabena trying to make the Industrial Revolution sound interesting again.

After break, we hit another bad patch. This time, it was the girls who were fighting. It actually started at break: while I was half-listening to Mandisa's never-ending story about Trevor, I noticed that one of my classmates, Sylvia, was having a screaming match with a Grade 11 girl called Tsidi.

'You're a liar and I hate you!' screamed Tsidi; together with some other things I won't repeat.

Then Sylvia burst into tears. 'It's not true!' she wailed, 'I didn't spread any rumours about what you did with Koketso last weekend!' – but Tsidi ignored her with a sneer, and all her friends shooed Sylvia away.

It looked as though the fight was over when the bell rang, but actually, it was just a pause between rounds. When round two began, Mrs Mabena was writing some idioms on the board. Squeak, squeak, squeak went the chalk. Suddenly there was a loud scream from the back of the room, followed by some angry swearing.

Our heads all swivelled round, but the girls took no notice.

'Leave me alone, you δ#çλ LIAR!' screeched Sylvia at Tsidi's sister Lerato, who sat next to her.

Lerato is usually a very quiet girl, and Sylvia is her best friend – but family comes first, as my mother always says. Lerato must have whispered something horrible to Sylvia. Now, right in the middle of Mrs Mabena's idioms, all hell broke loose. To the sound of swearing and grunting, they tugged viciously at each other's hair and clothes. After a few seconds, some others decided to join in the fun, while the rest of the class just cheered one or the other team on. All you could hear was squealing, wailing, clapping and whistling – the noise was unbelievable.

This was just too much for Mrs Mabena. I'd never seen her so angry. Her eyes bulged behind her glasses and her whole face puffed up like a frog's, so that it looked as if she might explode. 'BE QUIET!' she screamed. This did help to calm things down, because she didn't usually shout at us. Then she sent the four noisiest girls to the office. Finally she announced in a loud, angry voice that she had had enough of us, because we were just too wild. (This was a bit unfair, I thought. I was never wild – I just didn't listen.)

As a punishment, she was keeping us in after school for half an hour. At that, there was a chorus of moans and wails: 'But Ma'am! But Ma'am! My bus! My taxi! My doctor's appointment!'

Naturally that made Mrs Mabena even more furious. She reacted by doing something that actually changed my life. 'SILENCE!' she roared, like an angry lion, and we all shut up again. 'Now,' she continued more quietly, although she still looked irate, 'I think it's time we made some changes in our seating plan.'

I gulped, and glanced over at Mandisa; but why should she really care? It would only hurt me if I couldn't copy her answers in tests any more, not her. She still had me twisted around her little finger anyway, because I could be in big trouble if she told anyone about my cheating.

'Charles,' Mrs Mabena said grimly, 'swap places with Pinky. Natasha, swap with Lerato when she comes back to class. Tumi, swap with Eric.'

On and on it went. You are invisible I kept on saying to myself, trying to sit very, very still, so that Mrs Mabena wouldn't see me. For ages, it seemed to be working; about half of the class had moved, and I was just beginning to relax, when Mrs Mabena finally turned to me.

'Ah, Sindi,' she said. 'Perhaps you'll pay more attention in class if you swap places with Portia!' She pointed to the desk right beneath her nose, a sad lonely island of a desk with no neighbours at all. With one last look at Mandisa, who was now pulling a face at the idea of having Portia sitting next to her, I packed up my books, and shuffled miserably over to my new place. What on earth was I going to do? How could I possibly do well in my tests now?

Chapter Fifteen

'I'm sorry I'm so late!' I panted to Siya, when I finally managed to get down to the field that afternoon. Although Mrs Mabena had tortured us by making us sit in dead silence for 30 minutes, her punishment had worked out well for me – Mandisa was so keen to leave that she had rushed off to the bus stop without even noticing that I wasn't keeping her company as I usually did.

'That's OK,' said Siya with a friendly smile, waving to his friends as we left the field. My stomach did a strange flip. I looked away quickly, so he wouldn't see how shy I was feeling.

'Have you thought of anything we can do about the Mandisa problem?' he asked. I had to admit that I hadn't, but it was my lucky day, because Siya himself had come up with the most fantastic idea. As he told me about it, I grew more and more excited. Not only was his plan brilliant, but he took it for granted that we would carry it out together. That meant that we would need to spend a few hours together on Saturday afternoon. I could hardly wait; I had to stop myself from immediately trying to work out what I was going to wear. The only bad thing was that it might involve another little lie to my mom, but I told myself I would have to live with that for Mandisa's sake.

'Sindi,' said Siya as we walked back down to the soccer field, 'there's something I've been wondering about. Why does Mandisa have your phone? Don't you want it yourself?'

I swallowed nervously. What should I say? Confused thoughts swirled about in my head. I said, 'Oh, she'll give it back soon.' But then I looked up at Siya's open, curious face. Was I really going to lie to him too? It just didn't seem worth it.

'Well, the truth is,' I said, 'she's got my phone because she's been doing me a big favour.' To my horror, I felt tears prickling in my eyes. We were walking past the vegetable garden, and I stopped and stared intently at the tomatoes, trying not to cry. I was terrified Siya was going to laugh at me, perhaps ask me if I was hungry, or something – but he didn't. Instead, he just waited for me to talk again.

'Siya! I've been cheating!' I suddenly burst out. My voice sounded high and shaky. 'I've copied Mandisa's work for the past four tests because I just can't study any more. I used to know how, but now I can't. I just can't concentrate and I don't know why! And today Mrs Mabena moved all of us around and I'm not even sitting next to Mandisa any more, so I won't be able to copy her work! My mother will be so upset because I'm going to fail again!' Then I covered my face with my arm and cried.

It's a strange thing how bad you can feel when you have a secret. Telling Siya made me feel much better. The great thing was that he didn't seem to think my cheating meant I was a bad person. 'I'm sure you don't need to cheat,' was all he said.

'How can you say that?' I asked miserably. 'I told you, I don't know how to study any more. Before I copied Mandisa's work, my marks were getting worse and worse. I was failing.'

'You just need to learn how to study,' he replied. 'It's much easier when you know how. At my last school, one of my teachers told us exactly how to do it. I'll show you.'

'What do you mean, learn how to study?' I asked.

'Well, you have to be organised,' he explained. 'You need to learn how to take notes in class, and make lists of things you have to study. Timetables sometimes help too. You also need to learn how to write the test itself – there's a good way of doing it so you don't stress and forget everything. There are ways you can build up your confidence too. You'll see – it's easy!'

That made me feel even better. Maybe I could learn how to study properly, and everything would be OK. But then I thought about my phone again. I told Siya that I still couldn't ask for it back, because Mandisa might tell my mother about the cheating if I made a fuss about it.

He thought for a minute. 'I don't think she will. She's your best friend, and I can see she loves you. Anyway, maybe you should tell your mother what happened yourself.'

'*Tell her*?' I asked in amazement. 'Have you gone mad or something? My mom will kill me!'

'Are you scared of her?' he asked.

That was an interesting question. It made me realise that I haven't actually been afraid of Ma since I was tiny.

'No, not really . . . I just hate upsetting her since my aunt died. I know she's sad, and I don't want to make her any sadder.'

'Aren't you sad about your aunt too?'

I hesitated and then nodded. Of course I was sad, if I let myself think about it.

'Maybe you're sadder than you think,' he said. 'Maybe you need to tell your mother how you feel.'

'Maybe,' I said, but the conversation was becoming a bit too serious for me. I said quickly, 'The first thing we need to do is help Mandisa.'

He nodded. 'Of course – and we will!'

Chapter Sixteen

I cleared my throat delicately. 'Good morning, ladies and gentlemen,' I said in a calm and gracious way. Instantly, the room fell silent. Rows and rows of intelligent faces stared up at me in admiration.

'What a wonderful speaking voice she has!' whispered members of the audience to one another. 'She used to be a famous actress, you know!'

My soapie had begun an interesting new episode that day, in which I was a world-renowned biology professor. I was standing at the front of a huge hall filled with intelligent students.

'Today we'll be learning about the marvellous human body together,' I said. 'But first, I would like to touch on another important topic – that of how to study. Once, when I was a silly young girl, I didn't know how to study. But then thanks to my colleague and husband, Dr Dube' – I broke off here, and smiled at Siya where he sat in the first row – 'my life turned around. If I hadn't learnt how to study, things might have gone very differently for me'. I was just getting into the swing of things when I felt Dudu tapping my shoulder.

'What?' I asked grumpily, not bothering to roll over and look up at her. I was lying on the grass under the guava tree, enjoying the fresh air after finishing my homework. This tactless invasion of my precious space was just too much to put up with! Typical Dudu!

'Will you come and help me with something?' Had the child gone off her head? Surely she didn't need my help to dress up her silly dolls? I sat up reluctantly, and squinted at her in a slightly sour way.

'What do you need help with?'

'It's something I want to make for Ma,' she explained.

'Remember it's her birthday next week? Well, Mrs Xaba was talking about these memory box things you can make to remember people who die. I thought we could make one for Ma so she can remember Auntie Patience.'

'Mrs Xaba! Mrs Xaba! More fantastic ideas from the wonderful Mrs Xaba!' I said unkindly, but Dudu is very good at only hearing what she wants to hear.

'Do you know about memory boxes?' she asked me now, quite calmly, ignoring my attack on her hero, Mrs Xaba.

'Yes,' I said. 'I've heard of them ... But it's Ma's birthday. Won't a memory box make her sad instead of happy?'

Dudu just looked at me as if I were the little kid, and she knew everything. That child is getting a bit too cheeky these days!

'No,' she said, 'maybe it will make her sad for a little bit in the beginning, but I think in the end it will make her happy. Now are you going to help me, or not?' From the look on her face I could see very clearly which answer she was looking for.

'Why do my best friend *and* my little sister have to be these incredibly stubborn people?' I grumbled, as I sat up slowly. 'Once either of you has an idea in her head, no human being on this earth will ever get you to change your mind!'

But she didn't even seem to hear this, and I decided it was too much trouble to try to argue with her. I sighed and stood up.

'OK,' I said. 'I've still got the box from the shoes Ma gave me for Christmas. Do you have any paint?'

'No,' said Dudu, 'but I have a piece of old wrapping paper, and we can make some glue from flour and water.'

She looked excited, and suddenly, I caught her mood. Perhaps it was a good idea. It would shut Dudu up about Ma's birthday anyway.

'What can you think of to put in it?' I asked her as we went inside together.

Chapter Seventeen

'He's decided we must travel soon,' Mandisa was saying on Wednesday morning before school. 'We'll go to Paris first, then London – oh *no*!'

To my surprise, her endless story suddenly stopped, and she frowned sulkily. 'What?' I asked.

'Weeding!' she wailed. Then I remembered, and I sulked too.

Every week, different classes take turns to work in the vegetable garden at our school. That week it was our turn, and for the next three days, Mandisa and I were part of a team that had to waste our precious breaks pulling out weeds.

At least while we weeded, Mandisa didn't go on about Trevor all the time. Instead, we took the chance to moan with our classmates about how horrible Mrs Mabena's lessons had become. After her scary display of fury, we were all definitely a bit quieter; even Charles admitted that he didn't want to make her angry again.

'That woman! She's crazy!' he said, pulling a mad face as he bent sweating over the pumpkins. 'I'm scared of her!'

I nodded. 'I know what you mean, and it's even worse for me – I'm all alone at that horrible front desk! I'm so close to her that I can see right up her nose!'

'That's nothing,' said Mandisa. '*That's nice!* Just stop complaining both of you; at least you don't have to sit next to Portia!' That was enough to shut us up, except that we couldn't stop laughing.

The boring week dragged on. Would it ever end? On Thursday, I double-checked that Mandisa's plans for Saturday were still the same. Then I told her I was going to choir practice again, which left me free to run through the details with Siya after school. On Friday, I dared to tell her that I wanted my phone back. To my surprise, she didn't argue with me or threaten me at all; instead, she promised to return it after the weekend.

At last it was Saturday.

For once in my life I was happy to bounce out of bed at seven. I had a lot to do. I bathed, filed my nails, and tried out many different hairstyles. Then I tried on at least four outfits. Finally I looked perfect.

Very cool, I said admiringly to my reflection in the mirror. I wonder if I can get away with a little eye make-up?

And I did, too, because Ma was writing a shopping list when I left, and was too busy thinking about toilet paper and toothpaste to notice my eyes.

I felt so excited that I almost danced to the main road to catch a taxi. Siya and I had agreed to meet at Oasis café around the corner from McDonald's at a quarter to twelve. As I walked there from the taxi rank, I noticed that my palms were beginning to feel uncomfortably sticky.

Don't be nervous, Sindiswa, I told myself in my bossy, strict voice. You're a famous actress in the making, after all, and I forced myself to breathe deeply until I felt calm again.

Siya was already standing in front of the shop when I arrived. I couldn't help noticing him looking me up and down in an approving kind of way.

'Hi,' he said. 'You look really pretty!'

'Thank you,' I said, as casually as I could.

'I passed McDonald's on my way here,' he told me. 'I didn't want Mandisa to see me, so I hid behind this very big guy who was walking next to me, but I'm almost sure I saw her sitting with the pervert at one of the tables next to the window.' He glanced at his watch. 'Now that you're here, I think we should go and check again. It's just before twelve.'

Our timing was perfect. Just as we came close enough to see the entrance to the McDonald's across

the road, Mandisa and Trevor came out, holding hands. I gasped.

'There they are!' I said, and Siya and I quickly ducked onto the shady covered stoep of the cellphone repair shop, where they wouldn't see us. Not that there was much chance of Mandisa noticing anything at all except for Trevor. Even from across the road we could see how her face glowed with adoration as the flashily dressed, muscular man in front of her leaned down to give her a lingering smooch.

It was a strange feeling, as if we were detectives on a TV programme, tailing the crooks – but since it was my own best friend I was spying on, I felt slightly disloyal. But there was no time to think about it.

'Come on!' said Siya urgently. Across the road, they had finally stopped kissing, and with one last love-struck look over her shoulder, Mandisa began to walk dreamily in the direction of the taxi rank.

'OK,' said Siya, 'let's follow him and see where he goes now,' and we sauntered casually across the road, making sure that we kept him in sight as he strode off in a different direction.

Chapter Eighteen

For a guy with so much work to do, Trevor certainly wasn't in a big hurry. His first stop was the bottle store. He came out carrying a full plastic bag, and soon we were following him at a safe distance to a hairdressing salon about a block away. The salon wasn't very full when Trevor went in. We hung about on the pavement as though we were waiting for somebody.

Trevor made his way straight to one of the hairdressers. She was a heavily made-up woman with dyed blonde hair, who was busy blow-drying her client's hair. She switched off the drier, put it down, and turned to him, smiling. We saw him bending towards her. Then suddenly, to my horror, he had her in a tight clinch, and was kissing her just as passionately as he had kissed Mandisa only ten minutes earlier!

'Don't stare too obviously,' said Siya, looking grim.

Then quickly he told me to go inside and distract the woman at the front desk by asking how much an appointment would cost.

I nodded. My heart was hammering as I went into the salon. Actually, the woman at the front desk didn't need that much distracting; she was hardly what you would call watchful. She had almost finished painting her nails a very bright pink, but had taken a break to chat on the phone. She glanced up at me eventually, and sulkily ended her conversation.

'Yes, dear?' she said in a bored voice, and I began to tell her that I wanted to braid my hair. I was facing slightly away from Trevor and the stylist, but from the corner of my eye I could see that they were talking while she dried her client's hair again.

There was a slight pause; then Trevor bent towards her again. 'Till later, sweetheart,' I heard him say in his deep growl, over the noise of the drier and the soppy R&B song that was playing. I had to stop listening then, because the woman I was talking to was asking me something.

The next thing I knew, Siya had suddenly shot into the salon with his cellphone stretched out in front of him. It all happened so fast that everyone was completely taken by surprise. One of the other stylists realised Siya was taking a photo, and began shouting, but by that time Siya had already hurtled out of the door and disappeared. The stylists looked a bit perplexed, but Trevor took it very coolly.

'Oh, just some stupid kid playing a prank, I guess,' he said, as he turned to leave.

'Thanks very much,' I said to the woman at the front desk, as I followed Trevor casually out, but she had already gone back to painting her nails.

Chapter Nineteen

'You got it!' I said to Siya when he caught up with me a few minutes later. He grinned and nodded happily.

'A great shot!' he said proudly. 'But let's see what he does next.'

Trevor was about 15 metres ahead of us, by now. He seemed to be heading for the taxi rank.

'Maybe he's going home,' I said.

'Yes, you're probably right. Let's take his taxi with him, and see where he goes.'

'But won't he recognise us?' I asked doubtfully.

'I don't think so,' said Siya. 'Guys like him are far too busy hooking up with every woman they meet to notice anything much.'

He was right, of course. Trevor stopped and greeted two pretty women on the way to the rank, and once he was there he scanned the queues quickly, to see if he could see anyone else whose looks he liked. It seemed that nobody really took his fancy, so he jumped into a taxi that was going to a suburb not far away.

It was lucky for us that he chose to sit in front, next to the driver. The taxi was already filling up fast, and after a moment, Siya and I hopped casually into the seat right at the back, behind two large women carrying many bags of shopping.

After a ride of about 15 minutes, we saw Trevor preparing to get out, so we did the same. Then we followed him from a slight distance for about four blocks, until he arrived at a smallish face-brick house. An old car with flat tyres sat in the front garden, surrounded by bits and pieces of engine. Trevor walked through the front gate, pulled a key out of his pocket, unlocked the front door and went inside.

'Let's just hang out here, for a bit, before we put the rest of the plan into action,' said Siya. We leaned against a wall across the road in the shade of a big tree and waited. After ten minutes, we approached the house. Siya knocked boldly on the front door and then stepped back so that he was standing behind me.

A minute passed. What happened next couldn't have been more perfect – or more shocking.

'Yes?' said a tired-looking woman. Clutching her left hand was a grubby toddler with a dummy in his mouth. From the size of the woman's stomach, it was obvious that the next one was due soon. In the background we could hear the sound of some kind of match on TV.

'Good afternoon, Ma'am,' I said. 'We're market researchers finding out about families and the products they use. Would you mind if we asked your husband a few questions?'

'OK,' she said, in a reluctant, irritable way. Then she turned and shouted loudly, 'Trevor! Trevor!'

There was no reply. 'My husband is busy watching soccer,' she said. 'He'll never agree to talk to you now.'

'Never mind, Ma'am,' said Siya, 'You'll do fine!' With that, he whipped his phone from behind his back and took a picture of her and the kid, who spat the dummy out and started to wail loudly.

'Hey!' she said, completely bewildered, 'What do you think you're doing?' But Siya and I didn't answer. Instead, we turned and ran.

Chapter Twenty

'I'm sure these photos are all we need to convince Mandisa to forget about Trevor,' were Siya's last words to me that day.

I nodded. 'They're perfect!' I said. 'It should be easy now.'

But we were both wrong. Sometimes people don't like hearing the truth, and making Mandisa believe us about Trevor was really difficult.

Siya and I had agreed to meet near the soccer field at break on Monday. When the bell rang, I suggested to Mandisa that we should go down there.

'OK,' she said happily; she was still so delighted about her fabulous date with Trevor, that she wouldn't have cared if we had spent break in a swamp as long as she could carry on telling me how wonderful he was, and how much she loved him.

'Guess what Trevor gave me?' she had boasted breathlessly the minute she saw me that morning before school.

'I don't know,' I started to say, but before I could finish the sentence, she pulled out a brand new cell-phone, and waved it around triumphantly.

'That's why I don't mind giving you this trashy old thing back!' she laughed, carelessly handing me my precious phone, as though it were a piece of rubbish ready for the dustbin. Just for a moment, I have to admit I felt pleased that she was soon to discover the ugly truth about her stupid boyfriend!

'Trevor's taking me out dancing on Friday night!' she was saying now, as Siya came walking up. Mandisa frowned; Siya was already just a distant memory to her. But when he and I greeted each other and I told her we had something to tell her, she looked confused.

'You see, it's about Trevor,' I said, feeling awkward. 'On Saturday after your date with him, Siya and I followed him.' That was as far as I got.

'You *what*?' said Mandisa furiously, glaring at Siya. 'How dare you! You jealous, childish idiot! And you even dragged poor Sindi along with you!'

I swallowed nervously, but Siya stayed completely calm.

'No Mandisa,' he said. 'It was actually Sindi's idea. She's been very worried about you.'

Now it was my turn. Mandisa glowered at me, looking as if she would be very happy to punch me on the nose.

'I don't believe it! Is this true?'

I nodded. 'We have some pictures you need to see. We took them soon after you left.'

She carried on yelling at us, but somehow Siya managed to get her to look at the picture of Trevor kissing the hairdresser.

She stared at it, silenced for a moment. Then she began protesting, claiming that the man could be anyone – but I could see the shock on her face.

'It's not just anyone, Mandisa,' I said. 'That's the shirt he was wearing, remember? And there's another picture too.'

It seemed so cruel that it was difficult to go on. But I knew I had to.

'We met Trevor's wife and child,' I told her.

Her face was a picture of shock and disbelief. 'No!' she said, and I could see that even though she had hurt Siya, he felt as sorry for her as I did when he showed her the photo. As she stared at it, I told her what had happened, and about the way the woman we had met had called Trevor her husband.

I was sure that Mandisa knew I wouldn't make up a story about anything as important as this. But something inside her just didn't want to accept it.

'It can't be true,' she said flatly. 'There must be some explanation. Maybe that woman was lying. How can he be married already? He and I are supposed to be getting married, as soon as I finish school. He promised me, he promised . . .'

'Sometimes people just aren't what they seem,' said Siya, but Mandisa wasn't listening.

'I know what to do!' she said. 'I've got some airtime. I'll phone him! He prefers it if we speak at night, because of his work, but this is an emergency. I'll phone him right now and ask him if it's true!'

'Mandisa, don't,' I begged her. 'He'll only tell you more lies!' But she was already dialling his number.

Siya and I glanced at each other uncomfortably.

'Hello?' said Mandisa, 'Hello Baby?'

Suddenly the look of desperate, determined hopefulness on her face was replaced by a kind of frozen horror.

'Oh, I see,' she said. 'OK.' Then she switched the phone off and stared at us dully. Her face had gone grey.

'What happened?' I asked gently, but I had already guessed.

'He wasn't there,' she replied faintly. 'A woman answered, and said he wasn't there.'

There was a long silence. Finally Siya spoke.

'I'm sorry, Mandisa. I know you must feel terrible. I don't know if it will make you feel any better, but you aren't the only girl this has happened to . . .'

He tailed off.

'What do you mean?' she asked. I felt curious too.

'Well,' he said, 'Lots of girls fall for sugar daddies. And sometimes . . . sometimes bad things happen.'

He paused, as if he were thinking. Then he seemed to make up his mind. 'OK, I'll tell you what. Can you come to my house tomorrow afternoon?'

Mandisa and I were both slightly taken aback. Siya had never mentioned his home before; we didn't even know where he lived.

'Is it far away?' I asked.

He shook his head. 'Not too far. We can walk there. And I'll walk you back to wherever you need to go after that.'

'But why?' asked Mandisa in a low voice. She still looked dazed.

'I want you to meet somebody,' said Siya. 'I think you might feel better if you talk to her.'

Chapter Twenty-One

That night I couldn't fall asleep. I was glad that Mandisa knew the truth about Trevor now. But if she gave him up, would she want Siya back? And did Siya love her? Was I doomed to lose my chance with him, just because I'd protected my best friend? This was a horrible, tragic thought. I tossed and turned, trying to get comfortable in my rumpled sheets.

Then I began wondering what Siya was planning for the next day. It was very mysterious. Who was the person he wanted us to meet? And what if he only really wanted Mandisa to meet this person, and he'd invited me along just to keep her company? The main question was, *Did Siya feel like I did, or didn't he?* My thoughts went round and round, but they always came back to this question, and it made me feel sick.

When finally I fell asleep, my dreams were full of dark, twisting corridors that led to dead ends, and staircases that I was afraid to go up or down. It seemed even crueller than usual when Ma woke us up the next morning. I was so tired that for once

Dudu had to coax me out into the unbearably bright, noisy world, instead of the other way around.

'Come on Sindi,' she said sweetly, 'otherwise Ma will make our lives hell!' That made me laugh – she sounded exactly like me.

The morning passed by in a grouchy blur. All I really registered was Mrs Mabena's announcement in English that there would be another test that Friday.

Great! I thought sourly. Now what do I do?

At break, Mandisa couldn't seem to make up her mind about anything. One minute she was angry and sulky and refused to talk or smile. The next, she was thanking me for being such a good friend. Then she told me that Trevor had phoned the night before.

'I ignored his call, for the first time ever,' she told me, 'but then he left me such a sweet message. He said I was the light of his life. After five minutes I just had to phone him back. But somehow I didn't feel like talking. Mostly I just let him talk.'

She laughed bitterly, and then suddenly burst into tears.

'Mandisa, I'm sorry,' I said, putting my arm around her shoulder, but even while I was trying to comfort her, there was only the same old thought in my head – *does Siya like me, or does he like Mandisa?* It was all too much. I was relieved when the bell rang – even maths was better than trying to deal with all this drama!

Finally school ended and it was time to meet Siya at the front gates. It felt like ages since the three of us had spent time together, even though it was only a few weeks – and now it was strange to be walking along with the two of them. None of us said a word on the way to Siya's house. Once I looked up, and caught him staring at me, but he looked away quickly, and so did I.

Siya lived in a townhouse complex, behind a high brick wall. He pressed a button next to the gate, and after a moment, a girl's voice answered.

'It's me,' said Siya, and the gate opened.

Chapter Twenty-Two

We walked through a small, neat garden and up a few stairs. In the doorway stood a smiling, round-faced girl of about our age.

'Girls, this is my sister,' said Siya. 'Q, meet Sindi and Mandisa.'

'What does the Q stand for?' I asked.

'Queen,' she said, laughing and pulling a face. 'But my friends call me Q.'

We sat down and Q brought us some juice.

'What grade are you in?' asked Mandisa. There was a slight pause. 'No, I'm not at school at the moment," said Q eventually. Then she looked at Siya, as if asking him for help.

'Tell them,' he said gently.

'You see,' said Q, 'it's like this. At our old place, in Pretoria, I met this older guy, Tebogo. We had a great time for a while. Of course my parents didn't know anything about him. I was 14 when we met, and he could have been my father!'

'At first it was such fun. He used to fetch me after school in his Merc and take me for drives. And the presents he bought me! They were fantastic! Our parents are doing well now, but at that time they were struggling. My dad was in between jobs for a few months, and there wasn't much money around for anything more than food and the rent. Tebogo used to take me shopping all the time. He used to spoil me.'

'But then – then I got pregnant. And . . . my sugar daddy ran away! He said it wasn't his baby – he said all sorts of horrible things. He called me names to my own parents. My mother and father were very angry with me, and they hardly talked to me for ages. They still seem angry sometimes, even now.'

'After a few months, my big stomach started to show and the principal called me into his office. They aren't supposed to throw pregnant girls out, but he said I was a bad influence on all the other kids, and he suggested that it might be better for everyone if I left. Then I was just alone at home all day, with nothing to do. My friends were still OK to me, but I didn't see much of them. Lots of other people from my school were horrible, though. They used to laugh at me and call me names when they saw me in the streets. And all the old grannies in the neighbourhood lectured me and told me what a bad girl I was.'

'My parents felt embarrassed, because some of the people from church wouldn't talk to them any

more. They were happy when my dad found a job here, because they thought it would be better to start again in a new place.'

Q paused, and then said, 'My little girl is five months old now. She'll wake up soon, and you can see her. I love her very much, but looking after a baby is such hard work! I have to wake up a few times every night and look after her all day. I never get a chance to hang out with friends, like you guys do. One good thing is that I've had an HIV test and so has she. Luckily neither of us is positive.'

She sighed. For the first time I noticed how tired she looked. 'I've missed about a year of school now,' she told us, 'and I don't know if I'll ever be able to go back. My mom works full time, and she says I have to look after the baby until she's old enough to go to crèche next year.'

Just before we left, the baby did wake up. She was called Ketiwe. She was really cute, I must say – she looked a bit like her Uncle Siya – but I was very pleased that she didn't belong to me. We said goodbye to Q, and both promised to visit her again soon.

Mandisa was quiet all the way back to her bus stop. 'Bye Siya. Bye Sindi, I'll see you tomorrow,' was all she said.

'Bye,' we both said.

Then Siya turned to me. 'Can I walk you home, Sindi?'

My heart pounded. I looked anxiously at Mandisa. What was going to happen now? Would she be angry or jealous? But she was already staring into the distance, keeping an eye out for the four-fifteen bus. I realised that she had a lot on her mind, and none of it had anything to do with Siya.

'OK,' I said so casually that nobody would ever have guessed that I felt like a bird that was about to fly off into the sky.

That day I discovered something really great: sometimes things turn out just the way you want them to. My love drought was over. The most gorgeous boy in my school, the only one good enough to appear as the handsome Dr Dube in my exclusive private soap opera, wanted to walk me home from school!

Chapter Twenty-Three

'I told Trevor to get lost last night,' said Mandisa the next day. (Actually she put it a bit less politely than this.)

'He phoned me to try to beg, but I just said I wasn't interested in all his lies. When he realised I was serious, he had the cheek to ask me for the ring and the phone back!' She snorted with contempt. 'I told him to forget it. That stuff is mine now! He'd better buy cheaper presents for his next girl, that's all!'

One of the words we had to learn for English vocabulary at that time was 'resilient'. The new, studious me looked it up in the dictionary. It means 'able to recover from misfortune'. I decided it was a good word to describe Mandisa. It didn't take her that long to recover from the Trevor experience.

Within a few days she seemed fine, just a little more serious and thoughtful than usual. She admitted that meeting Q had taught her a lot.

'When she told us her story, I realised it could have been me,' she said. 'I could have ended up being a mother and having to leave school. Maybe worse things could have happened to me too...Trevor's the kind of guy who tells his girlfriends that he's faithful, so they don't need to use a condom. If I hadn't found out what a cheat he is, I'm sure I would have ended up in bed with him. Then I could have contracted HIV.'

Of course, Miss Resilient's serious mood didn't last too long. Soon a new name appeared in her conversation: Kamahelo. 'He came to visit with my cousins last Saturday afternoon. After I dumped Trevor, I asked my cousin Xoli for his number. Now we're sending each other lots of messages, once my parents are snoring away, of course,' she told me excitedly. 'He's *incredibly* hot! He loves rap music – actually he's a talented rapper himself. And so athletic!' She sighed, and half closed her eyes as if she were about to faint. Then she opened them wide again, and said, 'This one really is a boy, though! He's in matric with Xoli, I promise!'

As for my seeing so much of Siya, Mandisa really didn't seem to mind.

'You know, Sindi,' she said, 'I was never that crazy about him. He's just not my type. Such a goody goody! He's not bad looking, though!' She giggled to herself, then said, 'Not as gorgeous as Kamahelo, of course – but actually you two make a perfect couple. He's sort of childish, just like you!' I pushed her and she nearly fell over. Then we both laughed. I knew that she really did think we were childish in a way, but I was far too happy to care.

That Thursday afternoon, Siya and I sat under the mulberry tree, and he helped me to study for my English test. At first I felt awkward. What if he decided that I was actually too stupid for him to bother with?

'Are you sure you want to waste your time doing this?' I asked at least three times before we began. 'Wouldn't you rather be playing soccer?'

But Siya shook his head. 'I can play soccer tomorrow. Now, let's talk about idioms!'

So we did. And actually it was quite surprising how fast I could learn them if I tried. The grammar rules were easier than I thought too. First we went through all the work I needed to know for the test. Then Siya told me some more about study skills. We agreed that I would begin my new life of note-taking and careful filing the next day. (I was relieved – at least I had one more day before I became a nerd.)

'You can also work on your confidence before the test,' said Siya. 'Tomorrow, just before it starts, close your eyes, and imagine yourself doing really well.'

'I'll be so happy if I pass this test,' I said.

'You mean *when* you pass it,' said Siya. 'Being confident is part of doing well, remember?'

And perhaps he was right. The next day, just before the test, I spent a moment telling myself that I had studied hard, and that I was going to do well. We marked the tests ourselves, in class. I had to swap with Stanley the maths prof. When the test came back, I found I'd got 33 out of 50.

'Not bad!' I said to myself. 'Maybe I'm not so dumb after all. Maybe it's time to be brave, and speak to Ma.'

It was going to be difficult, but I had to do it.

Chapter Twenty-Four

After supper that night, as my mom was making herself a cup of tea, I told her my marks.

'That's good,' she said. 'I'm very pleased you've been doing so well.'

I took a deep breath. It was now or never.

'Actually Ma, we need to talk about that.' My throat felt tight. I took another deep breath, and the words came out in a rush.

'I did something bad at school . . . I knew you were worried about my marks, and I couldn't seem to concentrate, so I copied Mandisa's work for the last four tests . . . I'm so sorry Ma!'

I felt tears coming. I brushed them away and stared at the ground, waiting for my mom to start screaming at me, to tell me I was bad, to tell me that she was going to punish me for weeks and weeks and weeks. But to my amazement, the shouting never came. Ma was quiet for a long time. Then she put her arm around me.

'Thank you for telling me, Sindi,' she said. 'I'm not happy that you copied, of course – that was very wrong, and I would have been very angry with you if I'd found out from your teacher. But I'm very pleased that you told me. Have you stopped copying her work now?'

'Yes,' I said in a tiny voice. 'Siya's teaching me how to study instead. I didn't cheat in this test at all.'

'And look how well you did!' said my mother. 'Just keep it up! And by the way, who is Siya?'

So then I told Ma all about Siya. Of course it turned out Miss Big Ears was listening from the bedroom.

'You've got a boyfriend! You've got a boyfriend!' she said to me in a silly sing-song voice that night. 'Oh Baby! Oh Baby! Smoochy smoochy!'

'Go to sleep, you cheeky brat!' I said, trying to sound cross, and failing completely.

* * *

On Saturday, it was Ma's birthday.

Dudu and I had baked her a birthday cake the night before while she was still at work. It looked a bit funny when it came out of the oven – it was slightly sunken in the middle – but we decided it was better than nothing. Once Dudu had slathered chocolate icing all over it, it was almost perfect.

We had also put the last touches to the memory box. It looked beautiful. We had covered it in wrapping paper, and written our aunt's name on it, and the dates of her birth and death. Dudu had managed to find a piece of soft blue material to line the bottom of the box, and it was filled with special things. There was a photo of Ma and Auntie Patience when they were little children, and one of our aunt holding Dudu as a baby. There were birthday cards and letters she had sent us when she was working in Jo'burg, and a few ornaments that we knew she had liked. There was the AIDS ribbon made of beads that she had liked to wear, and her copper bangle. There was even a beautiful, perfectly round black pebble she'd once found for me when I was little.

'You know who would have liked this?' asked Dudu when we had finally finished.

'Who?'

'Auntie Patience. She liked pretty things.'

'You're right,' I said. 'And I think Ma will like it too.'

But when we gave it to Ma the next morning, I wondered if maybe we had been wrong to make it after all. She looked so sad when she read the writing on the top that I wanted to snatch the box away. Then, when she opened it and looked through the things inside, I saw tears in her eyes. I glared at Dudu then. I wanted to shout at her, to tell her that she was an idiot and that it was all her fault that we had spoilt Ma's birthday. But then Ma spoke. She looked tearful, but her voice was calm.

'Thank you so much girls. What a wonderful present. It helps me to remember her whole life, not just the time when she was so sick.'

She paused for a moment, and then said, 'These past few months haven't been easy. I've been feeling so sad, I just couldn't speak about her. I'm sorry about that – you've been missing her too, and I know you've also been struggling, even though you've both been so brave.'

There was a short silence. Then Dudu said suddenly, 'Mrs Xaba says it helps to feel better when someone dies if you do special things to remember them. Can we maybe do things to remember Auntie Patience sometimes?'

'Of course we can,' said Ma, wiping her eyes. 'What would you like to do?'

'Let's go to that park on the other side of town, where she used to take us when we were small to feed the ducks,' I said. 'She loved it there.' Dudu and Ma both liked that idea.

'How about next weekend?' asked Ma. 'Would you like to ask Siya along, so I can meet him?'

'Boyfriend! Boyfriend!' sang Dudu again. 'Sindi's got a boyfriend! Oh Siya! My darling! Oh Siya, I love you!' She rolled her eyes about, and waggled her shoulders and hips. I took a swipe at her, but she danced off and carried on with her song. That child is just impossible!